TO THE

MORMON
NEWLYWEDS

WHO THOUGHT THE

BELLYBUTTON

WAS SOMEHOW INVOLVED

TO THE

MORMON
NEWLYWEDS

WHO THOUGHT THE

BELLYBUTTON

WAS SOMEHOW INVOLVED

DEJA EARLEY

Signature Books | 2018 | Salt Lake City

For Henrietta Plum, who is bright and strong, and
Sam, who helped many good things come to be

Cover design by Aaron Fisher
Book interior by Jason Francis

FIRST EDITION | 2018

LIBRARY OF CONGRESS CATALOGING-IN-PUBLICATION
CONTROL NUMBER: 2018015320

CONTENTS

I

II

III

I

BUNNIES IN VELVET
ENSENADA, MEXICO, 1990

A vendor passed with a flat black box of jewelry
and my sisters left their towels and leaned over
his wares, clutching swimsuit tops to hold in breasts.

Younger than the others, I stood aside, wondering
why they didn't pick the pretty bunny earrings.
When my sister asked me which I liked best,

I pointed to the bowtied rabbits, and the vendor,
smiling, took them from their velvet niche
and held them to my ears. His hands smelled

of sweat and silver, and his fingers were coarse
against my cheeks. My sister gripped my shoulder.

¿Playboys? he asked me. *¿Si? ¿Si?*

HOUSEWIFE FOR HALLOWEEN

I.
For Halloween
I am a housewife.

I tow a plunger
at the school carnival.
Its rubber bowl bounces
off the asphalt.

II.
"Will you chop off my head?"
my mother asks. "Shake it out
into the spider plants,
then bring it back to me."

I slice my hands across
her neck.

MY FATHER PAID US TO KILL GARDEN PESTS

Snails didn't protest when we pulled
them from the lily plant, and their small
retreats into shells only made them easier
to shatter, thick insides mixed with gravel.

June bugs attacked the figs, hollowing
putrid cathedrals in the fruit meant
for my mother. We caught them in sheer
yellow nets and I drowned them quickly,
knowing my heart would pound in fear
until they stopped hissing. I used my heel
to pestle those still squirming in the grass.

Maybe white cabbage moths deserved to die
for tatting our nasturtiums into bright lace,
but they didn't look evil to me.
My net confused their wings with flashes
of sunlight, and my eyes softened and dazed,
watching the rhythm of external lungs
inhale–exhale. Before I could trap them,
they'd be gone, dissolving completely
in the burn of afternoon.

LASHES

At seven, bored and staring off,
I twirled a roach's carcass
between my forefinger and thumb.
I thought it was a piece of shoe,
a fringe pulled from the rug,
a stale crust of toast.

At last I looked. The body leaked white
and its legs lay on the hardwood
like a trio of jointed eyelashes.
I dropped the roach and stared at my hand.

The same room, the same floor, a year later:
I sat cross-legged, my skirt bunched around my waist,
examining my strangest anatomy: a set of gates, never closed;
a hollows with no apparent depth.

My brother walked in eating a peach. He shouted,
"Mom, Deja's playing with herself!"
I had to dissect the phrase: *play ing with my self*.
I had to track from his tone what I'd done, and hear my
mother call him into her office to explain.

For years I wondered at family dinners, at Christmas,
what she'd said, what she could have told me too, and
if he remembered it. I wanted to ask him if I dropped
the task or roundly denied it. I wanted to know
if I smoothed my skirt, if I lowered my lashes.

THE NECK OF THE VACUUM

I sit on the stairs,
toes spread through
green carpet I've
been sent to clean.
A revelation
pulses through me:
no one can make me do it.

My sister
is sent as enforcer,
and I make the mistake
of boasting my epiphany:
"No one can *make* me."

More amused than angry,
she holds my hands
to the neck
of the vacuum.

It's an awkward dance.
We force me,
shocked,
around the room.

THE CENTER OF A SWARM

The bees can't wait
for my father's
sturdy white boxes
and clean frames,

so they kiss my arms,
catch in my curls,
swarm with me at the center,
and I blink, feel like an eye.

Soon the elbow of
a lime tree bows to hold a hive.
The heavy bulb of honey
grazes the ground.

CHASTE DANCING

I was shy and half-disbelieving
as he pulled me behind him,
weaving through chaste dancing
in the church gymnasium, leading
to the dark couch in the foyer.

But now his tongue,
his insistent tongue,
presses against
the portcullis of my teeth.

It fills my mouth, evicting my own
tongue, a tongue that's
never traveled, never
intended to glide foreign terrain.

Our shared saliva overflows,
bathing our faces. Our noisy
mouths unsettle me. I wish
to breathe deeply, and can't.

But this is a kiss, I think.
Firstkiss, firstkiss, firstkiss.

I WATCH A COUPLE ON THE TRAIN

He wears black cashmere,
she wears black silk,
their bodies are backdrops
for new weddings bands—shiny as
tiny switchblades.

Reeking of airport carpet
and fast food breakfast,
I watch like I'm starving.

They kiss unselfconsciously,
their legs a tight-jeaned tangle,
one hand lost in dark curls,
the other macerating her breast.

They rest, breathe out, touch foreheads,
tease each other in French, and get back to it.

I try to turn away, to study a man reading
a picture book to his rubber snake,
a woman with a pinched mouth
pulling back layers of stockings to
scratch her scabbing ankle,
a mid-teen festooned in piercings
who can't take her eyes off the couple.

SEX TALK SUNDAY

I sit in a class of virginal twenty-somethings,
rows of polka dot skirts and shiny shoes,

waiting for a stern and nervous bishop
to deliver the semi-annual sex talk.

He stands, buttons his suit coat, unwraps
tissues from a bakery brownie,

and hands it to a girl on the front row.
"Pass it around," he says.

While it moves hand to hand, he preaches
the joys of the marriage bed, the dangers of being

alone in dark places with boys, staying late,
watching movies horizontally.

The mangled brownie returns to him
and he presents it, shiny with fingerprints.

Lowering his voice, he says, "You see,"
"who will want it now?" And I'm thinking

that it doesn't look that bad. I'm thinking
that I'd like nothing better than to lick
that brownie very slowly. Or better, bite.

MACARONI AND CHEESE

My roommate and the man
who sunk to one knee
with an engagement ring
after two weeks of dating
kiss and talk childhoods
in our living room.
Their kisses sound
like someone is stirring
macaroni and cheese.

She calls me in as audience
for a story about his pet frog
and she's lying on the sofa
like a diva—pale skin, dark hair,
head tipped over the edge,
asking if we have a can of olives,
complaining of her third
migraine this week.
He's kneeling
like he never got up.

He mutes commercials
on the Cartoon Network
and she swats his hand
from fussing with a zit.
"Now tell her," she says. "Listen
to this. He's just so cute."
As I leave the room, she covers
his eyes during a pantyhose ad.

Just before midnight, salt
and vinegar chips in hand,
she leads him to his car
where they'll deposit chip shards
in bench seat creases and read
their daily chapter of
Between Husband and Wife.

WON'T BLINK

After crossing Nebraska in the family car,
my sister and I catch fireflies in a field behind our motel.

She's nearing thirty, but we both feel twelve
as we trap lights in plastic cups and rush back to view
them in captivity. They won't blink in the Best Western
bathroom, no matter how long we watch.

My sister has a family—a husband and two girls—
but she's left them behind so she can play child again
to my parents in the front seat. We've stood together
at the grave sites of ancestors, picked mulberries
in Nauvoo, posed with a giant plaster buffalo.

The next night on the road, the fireflies in tall grass
look like stars that wandered down for a break
from their responsible loft. They glitter in streaks,
thousands of quick flashes. I squint, believing
we drive through outer space.

My sister has just talked to her husband
and she's looking out the window,
and I assume she's sad, though I'd never ask.
She tells us he was watching TV when she called,
and I'm young enough to think this spells marital doom.

I announce to the car, "I heard if you smash
a firefly on your face, it glows for at least an hour.
We should catch more. We should try it."

Then I'm sure it's what I want. If we could
catch them, crush them against our cheeks
and glow outside from their insides, I know
it will cheer her. I think we will be beautiful,
our faces streaked in brutal light.
I think my sister will be happy.
I think she will be mine.

THE PERFECT HUMAN

sings hymns in his sandblasted Humvee and thinks of
a girl in a red skirt. The perfect human met her once,
in sunlight too bright, while he waited for his taxi from
church back to base. He remembers her dark hair, an
enormous rose barely holding it up in a twist at her
neck. He arranges snacks for the convoy and longs
to confess his sins to her. Now he calls her from the
calling trailer and she's still in her yesterday. Forty men
attached to phones, calling home, and he calls her.
She tries to ask questions, but she's not the perfect
human. Look. She eats while she talks to him. She
cradles the phone and spoons stew.

COMMA SPLICE

The café door tones, announcing
that Casey with his chestnut curls
has held it open for me. I'm his
graduate instructor, we're here
to conference, and he's half a century
too young for his cane, but two
years older than me.

He leans. His tan forearm
shifts into stunning definition.

Over herbal tea and shortbread,
his comma splices vanish.
I am his humbled audience.
I ask, and he tells: Lyme Disease.

When he walks me to class, blossoms
swirl at our feet, the crosswalk bell
is a sweet song, and I am years away,
dreaming our tragic future. If his kidneys
failed and legs gave out for good, would
I still love this blue-eyed student?

I stand at the chalkboard, making bad jokes.
He smiles, and I know I'd hoist him,
amuse him, bring him sliced radishes,
remind him he once sat like a god
at the back of my class.

ARTICHOKE

Humming, I nestle artichokes,
preparing them to simmer.
I fill water to their hips, sprinkle salt,
and nearly forget to turn on the burner.

At dinner I teach him to bare
his teeth, scrape the fleshy edge.
He tries one leaf.

But I don't give up. I take a knife,
split the hair from the choke,
present him with a forkful of heart.

AVALON VALLEY REHABILITATION CENTER

Skin cancer grows on my aunt's temple,
black and wavy, like barnacles.

A nurse in purple scrubs feeds her coleslaw
while my father bustles like a new parent.

He explains the difference between her phone
and the remote. He folds a sweater, repairs

her glasses with a paperclip, while I
perch on a wheelchair, looking away,
rubbing the soft inside of my sleeve.

AGING

All afternoon the kids circle the yard,
backdropped by my father's blackberries.
They fight over baseball mitts, lean into their parents'
faces, smile at my camera over chocolate ice cream cones.

My sister wrestles her son into striped pajamas,
sends him to kiss us each goodbye on the tip of the chin.
Then she buckles him into his car seat and takes him home.

Soon my other siblings and their young families follow,
leaving for the rituals of bathing, story time,
cups of water, nightlights, locking front doors.

And now it's very quiet.
I sit up and read.
Only my parents in the house,
sleeping in the same bed, aging.

WHATEVER WOULD FOLLOW HELLO

In London, alone at a ballet,
I wear a wide hat
and sit very straight.
The man beside me is looking
me over, considering me, maybe.

I want him
to consider me,
to invite me
for intermission wine.
I want to stand at the window,
one heel propped behind the other,
flirting from behind my hat.

The trouble is, I don't drink wine.
And I don't talk to men who aren't Mormon,
lest I fall from grace, on my ass, lest I fall somewhere
I've never seen and can't imagine, but tonight I may try.

I sit stiffly, angle away from him, dart off.
And when I return from pacing hallways,
he's at the window with a freckled brunette.
She wears a long blue dress and tilts her head back.
Her laugh is like an advertising jingle and her leg is a
a long invitation, and the skyline out the window
appears a tiny perfect city in her glass.

SEDUCING STONEHENGE

Start with a small stone. Hold it for a moment,
dappled, cold to your cheek. Make eye contact,

but don't swank. No need to charm the brooding
posts and lintels. No need to whisper, confess.

You won't be fool enough to offer your heart.
It won't embrace you back. Won't caress.

Don't wonder who cuts the grass at your feet, or
why the freeway splits the Salisbury plains, or

how the grazing sheep can ignore their henge.
Listen to the crows tucked in their stone nests.

Watch the spiders pace their dewy webs.
Come away with lichen on your lips.

DOUBLE DECKER

The man on the double-decker bus
shouted *fuckyoufuckyoufuck!*
And my heart thumped, afraid.

He tipped back a beer bottle, shattered
it down the stairs as he got off, and the woman
with him didn't react to his spit on her face.
She followed in a miniskirt, middle finger flipped back.

Before all that, we'd passed a cherry-red truck,
enormous cages stacked in the bed, full of bright birds,
nodding on perches and tossing back beaks,
scarlet gullets rippling.

The fuckyou man had put his hand on the side
of the woman's head and turned it for her
so she would see the birds.
Look, he'd whispered. And they had both smiled.

At my stop, chunks of beer glass suggested themselves
to the soles of my shoes, and I saw more birds,
sparrows that could fit in my palm,
nesting in the OO of the bookstore sign.

I've lied. He didn't turn his girlfriend's head
and have her look. But if I didn't imagine
he turned her head, how else could I account
for feeling, when I saw the nests,

that his wet mouth, veined arm, and red t-shirt,
had somehow been beautiful?
That I was small. That we were all
shockingly important.

ALIEN ABDUCTION

You know the drill: bright lights,
threatening with elaborate forks.

Turns out they want to know
which color I could give up.

I can't give up red
because of your red couch,
and cardinals who look like
spare fire engine parts.

Not orange because I like
the startle of a close-flying monarch,
and perfect avocados rule out green.

They can forget about purple
because of the dress you like me best in,
the one with tiny black polka dots,
so not black either.

Stalling, I ask if, when I quit the color,
I'll walk around with blue tree trunks
or a pink sky, like in a used coloring book.
Or maybe that color would just mute, turn gray.
I carefully consider gray, whether I'd miss it.

The aliens mill and mumble, grow impatient.

HE'S NOT COMING

Enough with the swollen music.
It's quiet when it's over.
A train's wail wakes you.

You eat a frozen pizza
and three squares of chocolate.
Then you sneeze.

You drive home from the video store in the dark,
watching your reflection in the car window,
wondering if you're pretty.

Stop looking up. He's not coming
in with peonies.
He didn't hire a brass band
to say he was wrong.

MY IMAGINATION BEGS PARDON

Your cat hunches up on the rug
and retches. You go to her,
scratch her neck, coo your concern, and
wipe her mouth with a soft towel.
She struts off while you clean up.

I consider hunching up, retching.

IN THE HALL WHILE THEY TAKE CHEST X-RAYS

A tubby boy wearing green sweats whines to his father,
"But *when* do I get my snack?"

I'm impatient for the pleasant part too.
I stare at a silver cart full of gauze and bandages.
It's sleek and pretty in fluorescent light.

After they buzz around, sticking and stabbing you,
comes the part where morphine makes your voice thick.
Then I can sit on the edge of your bed, my arm across your torso.

As long as I don't get carried away,
as long as I don't swim around in the nurse's assumption
that we're something, that we're *we*.

BRILLO

If I had married my boyfriend freshman year—like I'd hoped—I'd be single again by now, and he'd be living downtown with his boyfriend. But I wouldn't carry around this innocence that I relish and despise. I wouldn't feel unopened.

And maybe my divorced friend wouldn't have said that thing that nags at me, that I think about when I wash quickly in the shower. Headed to the hotel hot tub, she said she hadn't "shaved"—all weighty, like our other friends would get it. And then she said something about Deja being like a Brillo Pad down there. I hate her for saying that.

AND I REMEMBER HE'S MY FATHER

I'm Mormon, and as such long
to scrub babies in sinks,
deliver vegetable casseroles to funerals,
find a husband willing to unclog drains.

I long fiercely.
Partly because we can't have sex
until it's time to make
pink-cheeked children.
And I'm getting older.

I dream my mother offers my father
as marriage material. He's done nicely for her
for thirty-four years, she thinks he'd do nicely for me.

And it's the event I've been mapping—
swishing skirts, rosebuds, and tall, polka-dotted cakes.
But quick, with just a slight nagging that it won't do.
Slight until the wedding night
when we're on either side of a bed, changing.

SEESAW

We walk easy through
a playground, unclear whether
to continue or expand forever.

You kick a seesaw; I sit on a swing,
remembering a playground myth, a kid
whose head popped off when he twisted
in the swing chains.
I twist.

Last weekend you took my shirt off, insisted I say
please twice, then peeled me, my arms raised.
Now I am ashamed.

For months I've felt like an art installation I saw once:
An exploding shed paused mid-blast, every piece suspended
with fishing wire. I've been blasting perpetually,
my shadows casting geometric violence against exhibit walls.

Tag my toe or take me to the ballet,
but when you nudge me in the park, I'm already gone.
I'm seven, at the beach, spinning
and spinning with my arms above me,
my parents walking ahead, their shadows elegant.

QUICK TONGUE

When I draw a bath, my cat thinks
I'm filling a water bowl.
She perches on the edge, leans down,
follows the waves I make when I
settle in, trills at them to slow.

Watching her, eyes green as sliced
avocado, I consider
pushing her off for hygiene's sake.
If our roles reversed, I would not
drink from a tub of bathing cats.

But I like her there, her white neck
stretched over my knee, disturbing
the still water with her quick tongue.

CADA REGALO PERFECTO
SONORA, MEXICO

Watching three orphans scramble on half-buried tires,
and the others grip pencils and crayons as if we'd given
     them chocolate,
I turn my purse inside out.

The altoids to a boy who sketches me on his new chalkboard,
looking up again and again to get the nose right—a Sesame
     Street oval.

My lip gloss to a slouching girl with a name I can't pronounce
who loves geography and sweeps the cloistered walkways
     every day.

The crackers to a sweaty kid I pose near at group picture time.
We are friends for the count of three.

My frozen water bottle to those we watch
through the back window of the bus
who jump and wave in the dust
and trash and shattered flowerpots
next to the technicolor Cristo in the dry fountain,
His robe magenta,
His arms open,
a plump bird perched in His hand.

THE OBJECT ITSELF

You're in the kitchen, rinsing
the translucent blue bowl I made
chickpea salad in. Your hands

are warm and slick, fuzz of dish soap
slipping from the backs of them.

Last night you held a button on my winter coat,
pulled it and rubbed it as if you were pulling
and rubbing me.

You were saying something serious, but I
concentrated on your hand, memorized it
tugging my black button.

It's the trick I taught myself when I was eight,
looking out the car window, sunlight flaring
cottonwoods, and I thought, You will
always remember *this* now, you will
always remember these trees.

IDEAL FORMS

A massive man sits wide
on a bench so his wife next
to him must angle away. His arm weighs
her shoulders, and she keeps tabs

on their toddler, a plump boy
wearing a striped leotard, pushing
a small wheelbarrow of plastic petunias.

Logistics seem suddenly disturbing.
How have these two opposite forms
managed lovemaking? I realize I
have no idea how things align.

Over dinner, I ask him—my boyfriend,
whom I've never slept with
because I'm quote–unquote waiting.

To illustrate, he stacks
two half lemon slices
and explains, it's not that way.

He angles two, spread like legs,
and thrusts another bright slice
between the others.

NOT YET

Still, yesterday we sat at lunch.
Servers and cooks gathered
at the door to watch a sudden storm,
holding their aprons and nodding.

He offered to get the car,
and I watched him cross the street,
hunched to cover his face, striding.

Slick from rain,
his car was covered in white blossoms
dotting the roof and slope of the hood.

I rushed out when he was still
down the street, U-turning.
Sorry, I said, climbing in.
I didn't think you would get closer.

THE SELF-FLAGELLATION OF THE NEW HOUSEWIFE

A black cat sits on the doorstep.
When I coo, it runs off.
The molten center of the planet
agrees I am a disappointment.
A volcano yawns.

Somewhere, a car wash burns down.
An orchid bows to a melting counter top.

"It's a snap," insists a shiny ant.
"Extend your pincers and take prey by the thorax."
But it's a big ant, the rainforest sort,
mouth like a tractor. I am small.

I make spaghetti and feel like a failure.
Washing dishes, I tell myself I tried. I really tried.

The members of the jury outside my window shake their heads.

YOUR EX-GIRLFRIENDS RUINED
ALL THE GOOD BABY NAMES

Forgive the litany. Forgive the barbershop-
sign inspiration. Forgive the walk in Central Park,
my pitter-pat over prams and kites and tiny shoes
the color of jelly beans. Forgive my weakness
for striped bellies, for onesied rumps pointed skyward.

A man teaches his boy to ride a bike, his hand
on the seat, the cheering, etc. And this tugs me,
opens a well in me, a center. Is there also a well in you?
Or is it only the original hollow, my plain anatomy?
At home, feathery green and bloom has followed us indoors.

Strange how purposeful lovemaking alters desire,
turns it edgier than pleasure, brim with risk.
And after, we sigh. It's not the pram we want, not the kites.
It's part you, part me, a name to whom we might say,
look, rabbits! and look, India! and look, the moon—it's yours!

OF THY WOMB

For Felix, who delivered and
died at home at 13.5 weeks

My Catholic husband prays
the Hail Mary over the body
of our baby, who has arrived at home—
without warning and far too early.

So early that Sam says
he looks like a boxer,
his tiny fists up to his face,
his eyes like black beads.

I ache for my own Hail Mary—
some mothering, mourning prayer.
I'm emptying, godless, thinking
of Her as we drive to the hospital,

of Mother in Heaven, wondering whether
half-organized souls ever dissipated,
split from her without warning,
left her in grief.

While I wait to be hollowed, I use Father
as a messenger to reach Her, if I may.
But perhaps it's no use.

She's not at my bedside, shimmering
in empathetic sorrow when I wake. She's not
there at the edges of me, or at the emptied center.

But maybe She's in the voice of the nurse who mothers
me back to consciousness and helps me sip water.
Perhaps She's in the water, in the stack of white pillows,
in the heated blankets tucked around me.

And perhaps She's in my husband's hand
as he passes it over my forehead,
gently as a prayer.

INTERFAITH DIALOGUE

You hand me a twenty while I'm driving
and I ask you to slip it in my wallet
and you sigh.

I think your sigh means exasperation,
means, "My God, woman."
When you reach for it, I snatch it back,
hold it to the steering wheel. You say,
"You always interpret my sighs as offense."

I punish you with silence.
The roads are empty and the quiet
radiates from our car as we drive
the streets nearing our house,
as we pass the Thai place we ate at once,
and only once, just after the miscarriage.

When we open the door, our orange tabby
is in the entryway, sniffing the air, rubbing
his face on the bookshelf, both glad
and frightened we're home.

I TEACH SIX-YEAR-OLDS ABOUT JESUS

A girl I've never met meets me at the door,
whines at my leg until I hold her. Thin arms,
thin mouth, a sour smell I overlook while fetching
crayons, glue sticks, snacks. She lifts her dress,
exposes the top of her baggy white tights, looks at me.
We both sing: *Faith is knowing the sun will rise.*
I sit next to her, tap her hands, whisper *no*.

Kyle, on the front row, holds a cardboard
box on his lap, a green scrawl on the lid.
It's his turn to toss the beanbag and recite
a miracle, but he stops, looks at me, says,
This is my box, like we must be introduced
before he can toss. He places it on the chair,
doesn't know the miracle, returns it to his lap.

Michael sucks on the wings of his plastic bat, swings it so
I'm showered in spit. "What's the bat's name?"
I ask, taking two fingers to slow it. "Jesus."
When I end the bat business, he howls and I hold
him like the *Pieta*, his sweaty back sticking to my arms.
I rock him, pray in his ear until he sleeps,
his tears soaking my blouse, his Jesus tucked in my bag.

OUR HILLS LEFT US

Our hills left us. Leveled out.
I don't mean to say that we flat-lined.

It was nothing so dramatic.
Just a settling, like smoothing out a wrinkle.

I think of that line of Plath's
about pears "fattening like little Buddhas."

And how I had felt like a pear.
You kissed my feet, the tops of them,

where the skin was loose and soft.

BIOLUMINESCE

We watched deep-sea creatures
bioluminesce in shimmering sheets.
Sirens outside, an orange haze from
street lights, strobe of the TV screen.
He held me and a manta flapped by,
graceful in marine snow, larger than a car.

And now a strange nonchalance, quiet car
rides and all that, laundry spats, creatures
tripping into habit, keeping both sheets
crisp, clean. Seven a.m., he calls from
Milwaukee and we talk through screens
and we know it. By the time we say goodbye

I'm licking a spoon of peanut butter by
the fish tank. I forgot to ask about the car
payment, forgot to say we're just creatures
tripping into habit, that his half of the sheets
was cold. The fish are darting from
one fleck of food to the other behind screens

of algae and glass. Maybe I need to screen
my calls today, lounge nude, take my bi-
quarterly mental health event. The car
won't start? I'm ill? Some creature
that I care deeply about ate dryer sheets
and croaked? If I can drag myself away from

peanut butter, perhaps I can keep from
calling him back. On the window screen,
a moth lands, flattens its wings. Out by
the mailbox, the newspaper waits. My car
is covered in dew and bird shit. You create your
corner of the world, right? We're issued blank sheets

and fill them? I pluck the moth from the screen,
hold it by wing tips. A car starts. I cup the creature
in my hands, carry it in, settle it on his half of the sheets.

TO THE MORMON NEWLYWEDS WHO THOUGHT
THE BELLYBUTTON WAS SOMEHOW INVOLVED

I.

I think of you two on your wedding day,
hands trembling as he removed your
pearled tiara and she loosened your
grandfather's cufflinks. Did neither

of you have a wry cousin in a tube dress
and tats, keen to play greeter for the new world?
Or maybe your cousin *did* try; maybe while
great-aunts swarmed, your cousin sidled up

to explain, tried to describe safe passage,
tried to tell you what a woman might
moan for. And you were so set
in your theory that you misunderstood.

Maybe you thought it good advice,
but you applied it to the wrong button.

II.
I can see how you'd be confused: the bellybutton
is decidedly erotic. Think of the belly dancer's

swiveling hips, the bikini's brash reveal.
A delicate crevasse, an inverted rosebud,

a cave of marvels, the torso's wink.
And the actual site of sex (you know it

by now, I presume?) does unnerving
double-duty, serving us so constantly

in foul capacities that it can seem
our least sexy locale, a soiled stripe

from front to back. But how
did you manage this particular confusion?

How deeply did you bury yourself away
from hip-hop and locker room brags

and amorous animal couples at the zoo
to maintain this pure but unenviable bafflement?

And what would you have done, upon culminating
the first undressing, if you'd discovered your beloved had—
confoundingly—an outtie?

III.
But now I am loving you both, imagining the tenderness applied
    to bellybuttons on your wedding day.

I think of the bride sprucing it fastidiously in the shower that
    morning, and of how the groom, her new lover, her only
    lover ever, must have lingered over it,

eagerly, tenderly, *insistently*. I hope you kissed it, and I hope she
    shivered with pleasure.

I think of my own fumblings, of how little sex resembled what I
    thought, which was mood music and candles and elegant
    lingerie.

I think of how, mere days into marriage, my husband went
    out for a toothbrush and I changed into long black satin,
    trembling,

exhilarated and unsure of the rules. I adjusted cleavage and
    smacked lip-gloss, crossing and uncrossing my legs,
    auditioning winning positions.

When he returned, toothbrush in hand, he didn't notice until I
    burst into tears.

IV.

I think of everything I didn't know was involved, how sex
    in marriage *is* sex, but it also concerns the price of car
    insurance,

and whose turn it is to scrub tub rings, and which smell wafts
    from the mudroom. It's about the rain outside hitting the
    sidewalk

in roses of splash, and a pair of polka dot rain boots or your
    husband's white dress shirt or a kitchen apron. What's
    sexiest is what's on hand, transformed.

You move the cat aside, brush away a fleet of toys, and hope
    you don't wake the baby. Quietly, quietly, you make of every
    mundanity a room,

and the two of you enter it. And this complicated alchemy,
    which encompasses every detail, can take years master, to
    reach virtuoso.

It's not a quick and thrilling drunken tumble into a stranger's bed
    and a stumble home. It's sex, then orange juice. It's sex,
    then mopping cat vomit.

It's a steady ramp, a passion no less promising if it begins in
    wild misconception.

V.
At some point you drift
for weeks, months, a year for each
baby, and still, when he comes
to you while you're finely
chopping celery, when he moves
behind you and his hands meander,
every cell is attentive. Your scars
and eye wrinkles, every button
of your blouse, every unshaved hair,
and every part that doesn't sit up
the way it used to, everything wants
to answer him, wants to show him
what you're made of,

wants to send him down
the proper shaft into the center.

A BLIZZARD WON'T BLOW

I think again that maybe I have cancer. I'm pretty as a
cancer cell: a mist and maze of burnishing blues. I try
to tell my husband that it gets warmer before it snows,
that a blizzard won't blow in nine degrees, and he won't
believe me. Why? he asks. And I don't know. I just
remember a creamy sky from childhood.

I haunt my ex-boyfriend's blog. He's gay, his last post a
pose of him and his boyfriend with cans of Orange Fanta
Soda. Fanta, Fanta, he says and shows his tattoo—
entwined cancer ribbons for his cousin and father.

Sometimes I want to crawl up the hoods of cars and
smash my cheek against the windshield, smear the
pane with skin-oil and tears. And sometimes I want to
make art from fireworks—blow stuff up until it's pretty.
And sometimes I want to take a bird that's died and
spread it out as centerpiece on my kitchen table.

We met a skunk in the evening, its gorgeous shock of
white all we could see at first, hovering beautifully over a
patch of pansies. Now when skunk smell wakes us, we
tell each other about it. We hold hands briefly and let go.
We sigh ourselves back to sleep.

OUR BED PROTESTS

Our bed protests beneath the weight
of my pregnant body, so I read
on the couch. An insect drops
onto my neck. I shout! And you rush over,

afraid my water broke. You tell me,
"Take off your shirt." I oblige,
and you push my heavy breasts
out of the way, pass your hands

over my domed belly and the slope
of my back, checking for centipedes.
Your moves are both erotic and not at all,
and you help me with my shirt and settle me
as if I were a child. I am glad

to be a child with ours so soon coming.
At midnight you stand over me, wake me,
and for several moments I have no idea
who you are. I wonder as you lead me

to bed whether I somehow spend
every night sleeping in my childhood
home on Palm Street with the mock orange tree
out the window. Dear husband, in that original

house, you would make no sense at all.
Perhaps this baby, once she arrives, will somehow
always sleep in the room we made her,
the moon lamp in the corner and the golden snails
on her bookshelf, and the windowpanes
shivering when city traffic rushes past.

BOBBING FISH

She arrives after all,
after too much waiting, and just enough,
and now she's asleep, head smelling
of Playdoh, and the two of us are whispering,
attaching a red balloon to her bedpost, guiding it
out the window so it's suspended in buttery blue.

We're standing in the doorway, waiting for her to stir,
when the cat jumps up and walks the four-year
length of her, and she wakes. And this is how I know
she'll be fine, exquisite even: when she sees
us in the doorway, she says,
"And what, may I ask, are you doing here?"

We're suddenly unsure of the answer
until she sees the tail of the balloon
and chases it to the window.
And then she's reeling it in as fast as she can.
It's a fat, red, bobbing fish, and she's laughing.

UPON ATTENDING A YOGA CLASS
WITH MY HUSBAND

It's a basic class, blankets and a dozen grey heads
on pillows, and soon he's snoring slightly. I reach over
and tap his rib cage, and we giggle in the back of the room,
our bellies trembling, the lights low.

When we reach to twist our imaginary light bulbs on and off,
I watch his hands, concentrate on them instead of breathing.
How long his fingers, how deep his palms, how shocking
that he has a body, that he exists separate from me,
from how I think of him as husband, from his laugh, his job,
his skills at dishwasher tetris, the way he touches me when I sleep.

We're on the floor moving like elephants, like cows, like our cats,
like the very deliberate and slow. His left hand stutters
when he realizes it should be his right. It feels like kindergarten,
like somehow the two of us—who are eleven years apart—
have skipped backward for an instant, joined each other
on the magic rug for stretching and naptime.

Then we're standing and lifting our arms high-high over our heads
and I can see his bellybutton, his small bellybutton, and he is
so young and I am so young and we both imagine we're floating
in shiny bright bubbles of light.

ACKNOWLEDGMENTS

Seven poems in this collection appeared previously in the following literary journals:

"Alien Abduction," as "Not Red," *Baltimore Review*, summer/fall 2008.

"Artichoke," *Sugar House Review*, spring/summer 2012.

"He's Not Coming," *Poet Lore*, spring/summer 2008.

"Housewife for Halloween," *Shampoo Poetry*, Mar. 2008.

"My Father Paid Us to Kill Garden Pests," as "Bounty," *Brooklyn Review*, summer 2007.

"Our Hills Left Us," *Lilliput Review*, Aug. 2007.

"Perfect Human," as "When the Perfect Human," *Borderlands*, fall/winter 2007.

Five poems appeared in three book-length anthologies:

"Bioluminesce," in *Fire in the Pasture: Twenty-first-century Mormon Poets*, Tyler Chadwick, editor, Peculiar Pages Press, 2011.

"I Teach Six-Year-Olds about Jesus in Sunday School," in *Fire in the Pasture*.

"In the Hall While They Take Chest X-Rays," in *Fire in the Pasture*.

"Of Thy Womb," in *Dove Song: Heavenly Mother in Mormon Poetry*, Tyler Chadwick, Dayna Patterson, and Martin Pulido, editors, Peculiar Pages, 2018.

"Quick Tongue," published as "Bowl," in *The Southern Poetry Anthology*, vol. 2, William Wright, editor, Texas Review Press, 2010.

Three appeared in *Dialogue: A Journal of Mormon Thought*, fall 2007 and fall 2011:

"I Teach Six Year Olds in Sunday School," as "I Teach Six Year Olds about Jesus in Sunday School."

"Sex Talk Sunday."

"Whatever Would Follow Hello," as "Intermission Wine."

Four were included in the online publication, *Psaltery and Lyre*, Oct. 2013 and Jan. 2014:

"And I Remember He's My Father."

"Interfaith Dialogue."

"Upon Attending a Yoga Class with My Husband."

"Your ex-Girlfriends Ruined All the Good Baby Names."

Six were accepted for publication in these additional online poetry reviews:

"Avalon Valley Rehabilitation Center," *Apple Valley Review*, fall 2007.

"Cada Regalo Perfecto," *Irreantum,* Nov. 2006.

"In the Hall While They Take Chest X-Rays," *Diagram*, 10:4.

"Not Yet," *PIF*, Dec. 2007.

"Of Thy Womb," *A Mother Here.*

"Seducing Stonehenge," published as "How to Seduce Stonehenge," *Product Twenty-one*, 2007

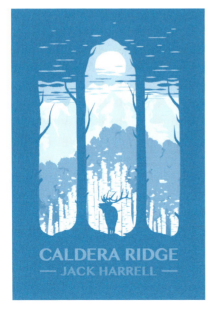

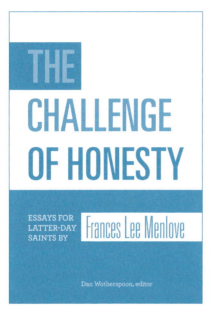

The Challenge of Honesty
essays by Frances
Lee Menlove
270 pages | hardback.

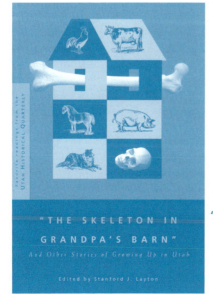

**"The Skeleton in
Grandpa's Barn":
And Other Stories of
Growing Up in Utah**
Stanford J. Layton, editor
264 pages | paperback.

A B C D E F G H I J K L M
N O P Q R S T U V W X Y Z
A B C D E F G H I J K L M
N O P Q R S T U V W X Y Z

The titles in this collection are set in Gotham Rounded, a lighthearted variation of the typeface by twenty-first-century American designer, Tobias Frere-Jones. The poems appear in Adrian Frutiger's Univers, a contemporary to Helvetica that is also known for it simplicity and versatility.

Deja Earley's poems, in their comic wisdom, demonstrate that we are all both small and "shockingly important"; that our hungers are both ordinary and ineffable, like "fireflies in tall grass" that "look like stars that wandered down for a break / from their responsible loft." This collection is a celebration of love and of our fraught, confused, and beautiful relation to the beyond.

   —**Angela Ball**, Professor and director, Center for Writers, University of Southern Mississippi; author of *Talking Pillow*; contributor to *Best American Poetry*

As Deja Earley delicately unravels the thrill and vulnerability of life, we are treated to a "forkful of heart." Each poem reveals the persistent innocence and discerning sensibility of a woman who candidly displays her private "cave of marvels" for us. In the process of reading, we discover and acquire an uncommon friend.

   —**Marilène Phipps**, author of *Crossroads and Unholy Water* (2000) and *Unseen Worlds* (2018); editor of *Jack Kerouac Collected Poems* (Library of America edition); recipient of the Crab Orchard Poetry Prize, Grolier Poetry Prize, and Iowa Short Fiction Award

"Life can only be understood backwards; but it must be lived forwards." So said Kierkegaard, and so argues Deja Earley's daring new poems. Her narrator doesn't lament this paradox, so much as celebrate the bumps and blows and bitter pills, the small deaths and titanic questions that come calling. Lucky passengers, we accede to her brave rowing. These are truth-telling poems that get under your skin and stay there.

—**Lance Larsen**, Professor of English, Brigham Young University; past Poet Laureate of Utah; author of five poetry collections, including *What the Body Knows* (2018); recipient of the NEA Literature Fellowship in Poetry

In this collection, the poet explores our often fumbling attempts to understand ourselves and to connect with others. Inviting us to join in her journey, she parts the curtain on the sometimes curious, sometimes sorrowful selves we inhabit in the privacy of blossoming, unspoken, and unmet desires. She at once flaunts and cross-examines the façades we put on and off like costumes as we interact with others. And she celebrates the heartaches and thrills of forbidden love, marriage, childbirth, and intimacy in its many shades and expressions.

—**Tyler Chadwick**, lecturer, Utah Valley University; editor, *Fire in the Pasture: Twenty-first Century Mormon Poets*; co-editor, *Dove Song: Heavenly Mother in Mormon Poetry*